Michelle + Jason.

Have a wonderful life
together.

Sue Griffin
September 2000

Also edited by Helen Exley;
Grandmas and Grandpas (1975)
To Mum (1976)
To Dad (1976)
Happy Families (1977)
What is a Husband? (1977)
Cats (and other crazy cuddlies) (1978)
Dogs (and other funny furries) (1978)
Dear World (1978)
A Child's View of Happiness (1979)
A Child's View of Christmas (1980)
What is a Baby? (1980)
What it's like to be me (1981)
Love, a Celebration (1981)
What is a Wife? (1982)

Published by Exley Publications Ltd,
12 Ye Corner, Chalk Hill, Watford,
Herts, United Kingdom WD1 4BS.
Selection and design©Exley Publications Ltd 1982
First published in Great Britain 1982
Printed in Hungary by Kossuth Printing
House, Budapest.

All rights reserved. No part of this publication may be
reproduced or transmitted in any form or by any means,
electronic or mechanical, including photocopy, recording,
or any information storage and retrieval system without
permission in writing from the publisher.

British Library Cataloguing in Publication Data
Marriage, a keepsake.
    1. Marriage – Literary collections
    2. English literature
    I. Exley, Helen
    820.8'0354   PR1111.M/

ISBN 0-905521-66-8

MARRIAGE
a keepsake

Edited by Helen Exley

Desire
has tied my hands
and love
has given me to you
as a slave
a willing
  meek
  docile
  abject
slave
who will never ask
for bitter freedom.

Rufinos

GIFT OF SIGHT

I had long known the diverse tastes of the wood,
Each leaf, each bark, rank earth from every hollow;
Knew the smells of bird's breath and of bat's wing;
Yet sight I lacked: until you stole upon me,
Touching my eyelids with light finger-tips.
The trees blazed out, their colours whirled together,
Nor ever before had I been aware of sky.

Robert Graves

ROMANCE

I will make you brooches and toys for your delight
Of bird-song at morning and star-shine at night.
I will make a palace, fit for you and me,
Of green days in forests, and blue days at sea.

I will make my kitchen, and you shall keep your room,
Where white flows the river and bright blows the broom,
And you shall wash your linen and keep your body white
In rainfall at morning and dewfall at night.

And this shall be for music when no one else is near,
The fine song for singing, the rare song to hear!
That only I remember, that only you admire,
Of the broad road that stretches and the roadside fire.

Robert Louis Stevenson

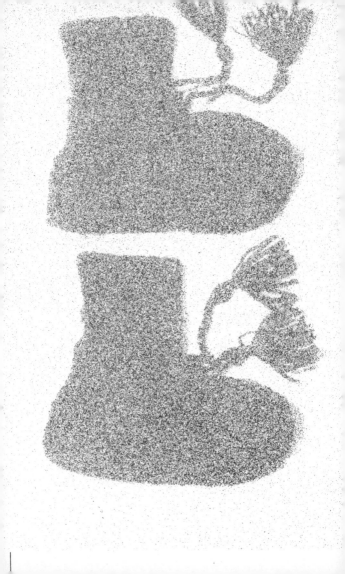

MR EDWARDS: Myfanwy Price!

MISS PRICE: Mr Mog Edwards!

MR EDWARDS: I am a draper mad with love. I love you more than all the flannelette and calico, candlewick, dimity, crash and merino, tussore, cretonne, crepon, muslin, poplin, ticking and twill in the whole Cloth Hall of the world. I have come to take you away to my Emporium on the hill, where the change hums on wires. Throw away your little bedsocks and your Welsh wool knitted jacket, I will warm the sheets like an electric toaster, I will lie by your side like the Sunday roast.

MISS PRICE: I will knit you a wallet of forget-me-not blue, for the money to be comfy. I will warm your heart by the fire so that you can slip it in under your vest when the shop is closed.

MR EDWARDS: Myfanwy, Myfanwy, before the mice gnaw at your bottom drawer will you say

MISS PRICE: Yes, Mog, yes, Mog, yes, yes, yes.

MR EDWARDS: And all the bells of the tills of the town shall ring for our wedding.

Dylan Thomas

A SLICE OF WEDDING CAKE

Why have such scores of lovely, gifted girls
    Married impossible men?
Simple self-sacrifice may be ruled out,
    And missionary endeavour, nine times out of ten.

Repeat 'impossible men': not merely rustic,
    Foul-tempered or depraved
(Dramatic foils chosen to show the world
    How well women behave, and always have behaved).

Impossible men: idle, illiterate,
    Self-pitying, dirty, sly,
For whose appearance even in City parks
    Excuses must be made to casual passers-by.

Has God's supply of tolerable husbands
    Fallen, in fact, so low?
Or do I always over-value woman
    At the expense of man?
                Do I?
                        It might be so.

Robert Graves

EPITHALAMION

Singing, today I married my white girl
beautiful in a barley field.
Green on thy finger a grass blade curled,
so with this ring I thee wed, I thee wed,
and send our love to the loveless world
of all the living and all the dead.

Now, no more than vulnerable human,
we, more than one, less than two,
are nearly ourselves in a barley field –
and only love is the rent that's due
though the bailiffs of time return anew
to all the living but not the dead.

Shipwrecked, the sun sinks down harbours
of a sky, unloads its liquid cargoes
of marigolds, and I and my white girl

lie still in the barley – who else wishes
to speak, what more can be said
by all the living against all the dead?

Come then all you wedding guests:
green ghost of trees, gold of barley,
you blackbird priests in the field,
you wind that shakes the pansy head
fluttering on a stalk like a butterfly;
come the living and come the dead.

Listen flowers, birds, winds, worlds,
tell all today that I married
more than a white girl in the barley –
for today I took to my human bed
flower and bird and wind and world,
and all the living and all the dead.

Dannie Abse

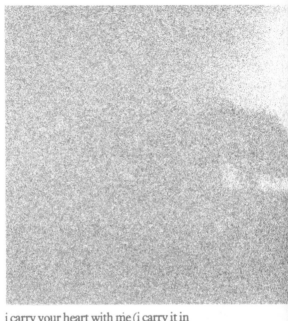

i carry your heart with me (i carry it in
my heart) i am never without it (anywhere
i go you go, my dear; and whatever is done
by only me is your doing, my darling)

                              i fear
no fate (for you are my fate, my sweet) i want
no world (for beautiful you are my world, my true)
and it's you are whatever a moon has always meant
and whatever a sun will always sing is you

here is the deepest secret nobody knows
(here is the root of the root and the bud of the bud
and the sky of the sky of a tree called life; which grows
higher than soul can hope or mind can hide)
and this is the wonder that's keeping the stars apart

i carry your heart (i carry it in my heart)

e. e. cummings

Antonio, that good fellow,
has recently got married
and is happy with his wife,
for there is no one lovelier,
sweeter, and more faithful,
more filled with affection,
more free of duplicity,
gentler of character,
easier to seduce –

Rubén Darío

THE AUTHOR TO HIS WIFE,
OF A WOMAN'S ELOQUENCE

My Mall, I mark that when you mean to prove me
To buy a velvet gown, or some rich border,
Thou call'st me good sweet heart, thou swear'st to
  love me,
Thy locks, thy lips, thy looks, speak all in order,
Thou think'st, and right thou think'st, that these
  do move me,
That all these severally thy suit do further:
  But shall I tell thee what most thy suit advances?
  Thy fair smooth words? no, no, thy fair smooth
    haunches.

Sir John Harington

Extract from WHO

Who can I
spend my life
with
Who can I
listen to Georges Brassens
singing
'*Les amoureux des bancs publiques*
with
Who can I
go to Paris with
getting drunk at night with
tall welldressed spades
Who can I
quarrel with
outside chipshops
in sidestreets
on landings
Who else
can sing along with Shostakovitch
Who else
would sign a Christmas card
'*Cannonball*'
Who else
can work the bathroom geyser
Who else
drinks as much bitter

Who else
makes all my favourite meals
except the ones I make
myself
Who else
would bark back at dogs
in the moonlit lamplight streets
. . . who
came in from the sun
the day
the world went spinning away
from me
who
doesn't wash the clothes I always want
who
spends my money
who
wears my dressing gown
and always leaves the sleeves turned up
who
makes me feel
as empty as the house does
when she's not there
who
else
but
you

Adrian Henri, for Joyce

THAT'S ENOUGH FOR ME

If I can make you cry
If I can fill your eyes with pleasure
Just by holding you
In the early hours of mornin'
When the day that lies ahead's
Not quite begun

... If I can make you smile
If I can move you close
To laughter with a word or two
When your day's been filled with strangers
And the castles that you build
All tumble down

Oh well, that's enough for me
That's all the hero I need to be
I smile to think of you and me
You and I
And how our pleasure makes you cry

Paul Williams

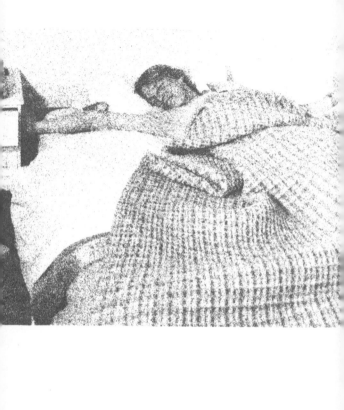

HAPPINESS

lying in bed ofa weekdaymorning
Autumn
and the trees
none the worse for it.
Youve just got up
to make tea toast and a bottle
leaving pastures warm
for me to stretch into

in his cot
the littlefella
outsings the birds

Plenty of honey in the cupboard.
Nice.

Roger McGough

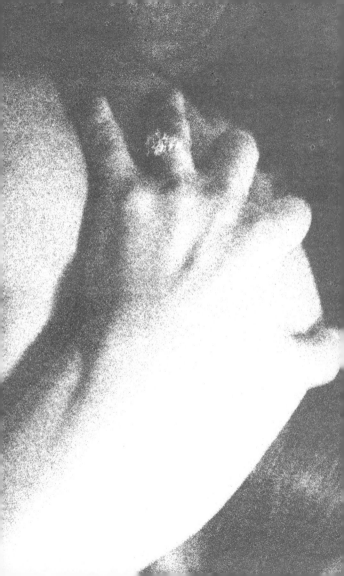

A LOVE POEM

—— whose body has opened
Night after night
Harbouring loneliness,
Cancelling the doubts
Of which I am made,
Night after night
Taste me upon you.

Night and then again night,
And in your movements
The bed's shape is forgotten.
Sinking through it I follow,
Adrift on the taste of you.

I cannot speak clearly about you.
Night and then again night,
And after a night beside you
Night without you is barren.

I have never discovered
What alchemy makes
Your flesh different from the rest,
Nor why all that's commonplace
Comes to seem unique,

And though down my spine one answer leaks
It does not bother to explain itself.

Brian Patten

We used to strike sparks
off each other.
Our eyes would meet
or our hands,
and the blue lightning of love
would sear the air.

Now we are soft.
We loll
in the same sleepy bed,
skin of my skin,
hair of my head,
sweat of my sweat –
you are kin,
brother & mother
all in one,
husband, lover,
muse & comforter;
I love you even better
without sparks.

We are pebbles in the tide
rolling against each other.
The surf crashes above us;
the irregular pulse
of the ocean
drives our blood,
but we are growing smooth
against each other.

Are we living happily ever after?
What will happen
to my love of cataclysms?
My love of sparks & fire,
my love of ice?

Fellow pebble,
let us roll
against each other.
Perhaps the sparks are clearer
under water.

Erica Jong, 'Living Happily Ever After'

A BIRTHDAY POEM FOR MADELEINE

It was at first merely the inconvenience
– Children, we thought, would interrupt our love,
Our lovemaking, thwart our careers,
Interfere with plans for foreign travel,
Leave us less money for drink and cigarettes,
And generally be a bloody nuisance.

Then, almost without our noticing it,
There the three enchanters were, and we
Were more in love than ever, and we told
Childless friends to follow our example.

But now – three tall daughters growing taller
Every day – who am I to boast I bear
Such tall and triple responsibility?
I should be frightened, I should run away
To sea, or to some childless woman's arms,
Or to writing poems in a lonely room.

Then I see your smile upon the pillow,
And, forgetting inconvenience, responsibility,
I answer as I can to your sweet asking,
And only hope these girls deserve their mother.

T. Harri Jones

WOMAN

Woman I can hardly express
My mixed emotions at my thoughtlessness
After all I'm forever in your debt
And woman I will try to express
My inner feelings and thankfulness
For showing me the meaning of success ooh well
Woman I know you understand
The little child inside the man
Please remember my life is in your hands
And woman hold me close to your heart
However distant don't keep us apart
After all it is written in the stars ooh well
Woman please let me explain
I never meant to cause you sorrow or pain
So let me tell you again and again and again
    (I love you now and forever)

John Lennon

hn and Yoko Ono Lennon

IN SEPTEMBER

Again the golden month, still
Favourite, is renewed;
Once more I'd wind it in a ring
About your finger, pledge myself
Again, my love, my shelter,
My good roof over me,
My strong wall against winter.

Be bread upon my table still
And red wine in my glass; be fire
Upon my hearth. Continue,
My true storm door, continue
To be sweet lock to my key;
Be wife to me, remain
The soft silk on my bed.

Be morning to my pillow,
Multiply my joy. Be my rare coin
For counting, my luck, my
Granary, my promising fair
Sky, my star, the meaning
Of my journey. Be, this year too,
My twelve months long desire.

John Ormond

PART OF PLENTY

When she carries food to the table and stoops down
– Doing this out of love – and lays soup with its good
Tickling smell, or fry winking from the fire
And I look up, perhaps from a book I am reading
Or other work: there is an importance of beauty
Which can't be accounted for by there and then,
And attacks me, but not separately from the welcome
Of the food, or the grace of her arms.

When she puts a sheaf of tulips in a jug
And pours in water and presses to one side
The upright stems and leaves that you hear creak,
Or loosens them, or holds them up to show me,
So that I see the tangle of their necks and cups
With the curls of her hair, and the body they are held
Against, and the stalk of the small waist rising
And flowering in the shape of breasts;
Whether in the bringing of the flowers or the food
She offers plenty, and is part of plenty,
And whether I see her stooping, or leaning with the
    flowers,
What she does is ages old, and she is not simply,
No, but lovely in that way.

Bernard Spencer

CAN'T HELP LOVIN' DAT MAN

Mah man is shiftless
An' good fo' nothin' too,
He's mah man jes' de same.
He's never near me when dere is work to
do.

. . . Fish got to swim and birds got to fly,
I got to love one man till I die,
Can't help lovin' dat man of mine.
Tell me he's lazy, tell me he's slow,
Tell me I'm crazy, maybe I know.
Can't help lovin' dat man of mine!

. . . When he goes away,
Dat's a rainy day,
An' when he comes back dat day is fine,
The sun will shine.
He can come home as late as can be,
Home without him ain't no home to me,
Can't help lovin' dat man of mine!

Oscar Hammerstein 2nd

How wise I am to have instructed the butler to instruct
the first footman to instruct the second footman to
instruct the doorman to order my carriage;
I am about to volunteer a definition of marriage.
Just as I know that there are two Hagens, Walter and
Copen,
I know that marriage is a legal and religious alliance
entered into by a man who can't sleep with the window
shut and a woman who can't sleep with the window open.
Moreover, just as I am unsure of the difference between
flora and fauna and flotsam and jetsam,
I am quite sure that marriage is the alliance of two people
one of whom never remembers birthdays and the other
never forgetsam,
And he refuses to believe there is a leak in the water pipe
or the gas pipe and she is convinced she is about to
asphyxiate or drown,
And she says Quick get up and get my hairbrushes off the
windowsill, it's raining in, and he replies Oh they're all
right, it's only raining straight down.
That is why marriage is so much more interesting than
divorce,
Because it's the only known example of the happy
meeting of the immovable object and the irresistible force.
So I hope husbands and wives will continue to debate and
combat over everything debatable and combatable,
Because I believe a little incompatibility is the spice of life,
particularly if he has income and she is pattable.

Ogden Nash, 'I do, I will, I have'

HUSBAND TO WIFE: PARTY GOING

Turn where the stairs bend
In this other house; statued in other light,
Allow the host to ease you from your coat.
Stand where the stairs bend,
A formal distance from me, then descend
With delicacy conscious but not false
And take my arm, as if I were someone else.

Tonight, in a strange room
We will be strangers: let our eyes be blind
To all our customary stances –
Remark how well I'm groomed,
I will explore your subtly-voiced nuances
Where delicacy is conscious but not false,
And take your hand, as if you were someone else.

Home forgotten, rediscover
Among chirruping of voices, chink of glass,
Those simple needs that turned us into lovers,
How solitary was the wilderness
Until we met, took leave of hosts and guests,
And with delicate consciousness of what was false
Walked off together, as if there were no one else.

Brian Jones

A SINGLE FLOWER

I can't talk to rocks
and trees, but I talk
to myself too much.
I'll grow a single flower
in my garden
and give it to my wife.
Is a man any less a poet
because he stays home
with his wife and children,
or is poetry always written
by someone wild?

This is not a poem
about marriage.
It's a poem about love.
I have lived with one woman
for nearly twelve years,
and although I only write
a short poem
each time we're together,
I also add a line
to a longer poem
for a later year.

Jim Burns

QUIET SONG
IN TIME OF CHAOS

Here
Is home.
Is peace.
Is quiet.

Here
Is love
That sits by the hearth
And smiles into the fire,
As into a memory
Of happiness,
As into the eyes
Of quiet.

Here
Is faith
That can be silent.
It is not afraid of silence.
It knows happiness
Is a deep pool
Of quiet.

Here
Sadness, too,
Is quiet.
Is the earth's sadness
On autumn afternoons
When days grow short,
And the year grows old,
When frost is in the air,
And suddenly one notices
Time's hair
Has grown whiter.

Here?
Where is here?
But you understand.
In my heart
Within your heart
Is home.
Is peace.
Is quiet.

Eugene O'Neill
To Carlotta on her birthday

Then Almitra spoke again and said, And what
of Marriage, master?
And he answered saying:
You were born together, and together you
shall be for evermore.
You shall be together when the white wings of
death scatter your days.
Aye, you shall be together even in the silent
memory of God.
But let there be spaces in your togetherness.
And let the winds of the heavens dance
between you.

Love one another, but make not a bond of
love:
Let it rather be a moving sea between the
shores of your souls.
Fill each other's cup but drink not from one
cup.
Give one another of your bread but eat not
from the same loaf.
Sing and dance together and be joyous, but let
each one of you be alone,
Even as the strings of a lute are alone though
they quiver with the same music.

Give your hearts, but not into each other's
keeping.
For only the hand of Life can contain your
hearts.
And stand together yet not too near together:
For the pillars of the temple stand apart,
And the oak tree and the cypress grow not in
each other's shadow.

Kahlil Gibran, 'The Prophet'

TRUST

Oh we've got to trust
one another again
in some essentials.

Not the narrow little
bargaining trust
that says: I'm for you
if you'll be for me.

But a bigger trust,
a trust of the sun
that does not bother
about moth and rust,
and we see it shining
in one another.

Oh don't you trust me,
don't burden me
with your life and affairs; don't thrust me
into your cares.

But I think you may trust
the sun in me
that glows with just
as much glow as you see
in me, and no more.

But if it warms
your heart's quick core
why then trust it, it forms
one faithfulness more.

And be, oh be
a sun to me,
not a weary, insistent
personality

but a sun that shines
and goes dark, but shines
again and entwines
with the sunshine in me

till we both of us
are more glorious
and more sunny.

D. H. Lawrence

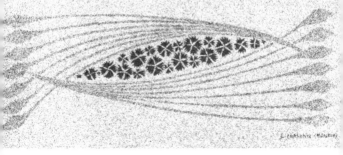

Love is something far more than desire for sexual intercourse; it is the principal means of escape from the loneliness which affects most men and women throughout the greater part of their lives. There is a deep-seated fear, in most people, of the cold world and the possible cruelty of the herd; there is a longing for affection, which is often concealed by roughness, boorishness or a bullying manner in men, and by nagging and scolding in women. Passionate mutual love while it lasts puts an end to this feeling; it breaks down the hard walls of the ego, producing a new being composed of two in one. Nature did not construct human beings to stand alone, since they cannot fulfil her biological purpose except with the help of another; and civilized people cannot fully satisfy their sexual instinct without love. The instinct is not completely satisfied unless a man's whole being, mental quite as much as physical, enters into the relation. Those who have never known the deep intimacy and the intense companionship of mutual love have missed the best thing that life has to give; unconsciously, if not consciously, they feel this, and the resulting disappointment inclines them towards envy, oppression and cruelty. To give due place to passionate love should be therefore a matter which concerns the sociologist, since, if they miss this experience, men and women cannot attain their full stature, and cannot feel towards the rest of the world that kind of generous warmth without which their social activities are pretty sure to be harmful.   *Bertrand Russell*

Cuckoos lead Bohemian lives,
They fail as husbands and as wives,
Therefore they cynically disparage
Everybody else's marriage. *Ogden Nash*

In villages in Pakistan, a prospective bridegroom is
brought before relatives of the bride, who insult
him with every known invective. The theory is that,
if he can take that, he has nothing to fear from what
the bride will say later. *Robin Ray*

Marriage is the best state for man in general; and
every man is a worse man in proportion as he is
unfit for the married state. *Johnson*

It is as absurd to say that a man can't love one
woman all the time as it is to say that a violinist
needs several violins to play the same piece of
music. *Honore de Balzac*

Marriage is the only adventure open to the
cowardly. *Voltaire*

Marriage is popular because it combines the
maximum of temptation with the maximum of
opportunity. *George Bernard Shaw*

Marriage: A sort of friendship recognized by the
police. *Robert Louis Stevenson*

Let me not to the marriage of true minds
Admit impediments. Love is not love
Which alters when it alteration finds,
Or bends with the remover to remove:
O, no! It is an ever fixed mark,
That looks on tempests and is never shaken,
It is the star to every wandering bark,
Whose worth's unknown, although his height be taken
Love's not Time's fool, though rosy lips and cheeks
Within his bending sickle's compass come;
Love alters not, with his brief hours and weeks,
But bears it out even to the edge of doom.
If this be error and upon me proved,
I never writ, nor no man ever loved.

William Shakespeare

A DEDICATION TO MY WIFE

To whom I owe the leaping delight
That quickens my senses in our wakingtime
And the rhythm that governs the repose of our
sleepingtime,
    The breathing in unison

Of lovers whose bodies smell of each other
Who think the same thoughts without need of
speech
And babble the same speech without need of
meaning.

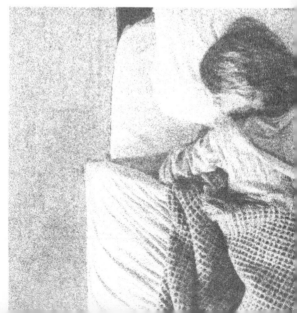

No peevish winter wind shall chill
No sullen tropic sun shall wither
The roses in the rose-garden which is ours and ours
only

But this dedication is for others to read:
These are private words addressed to you in public.

T. S. Eliot

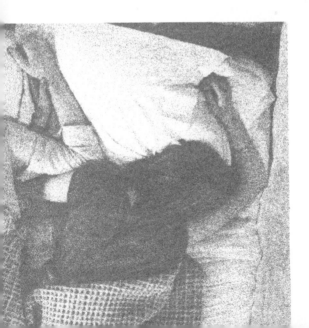

You have time for everything,
tireless and good, severe and comforting,
sorrow and song, day and night
always by my side,
asleep, in dreams,
in crowds, alone.
You have time for everything,
to stand and stroke my hair,
to go through piles of books,
essays and compositions, notes . . .
time for marking, time for reading,
time for working in the lab,
time for each child of all the hundreds
of autobiographies
of which you write a page.

Among the essays on the shelves,
piled high with books and notes,
our little girl listens to you
dreamy eyed as you tell the story of Snow White
and the seven kind dwarfs.

You have time for everything,
there where you sit among your formulas,
planning your lessons for the coming week,
tireless and good, the very heart of life.

Ion Horea

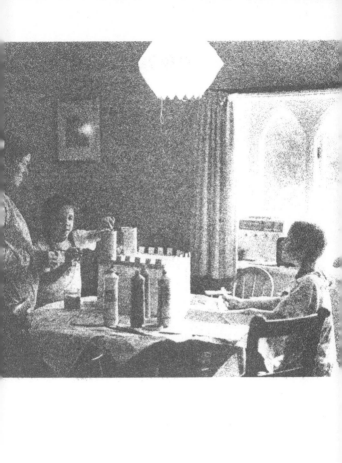

HELP

... When I was younger, so much younger than
today,
I never needed anybody's help in any way,
but now these days are gone I'm not so self
assured,
now I find I've changed my mind I've
opened up the doors.
... And now my life has changed in oh so many
ways,
my independence seems to vanish in the haze,
But ev'ry now and then I feel so insecure,
I know that I just need you like I've never done
before.
Help me if you can I'm feeling down
And I do appreciate you being 'round
Help me get my feet back on the ground
Won't you please please help me.

John Lennon and Paul McCartney

Paul and Linda McCartney

it may not always be so; and i say
that if your lips, which i have loved, should touch
another's, and your dear strong fingers clutch
his heart, as mine in time not far away;
if on another's face your sweet hair lay
in such a silence as i know, or such
great writhing words as, uttering overmuch,
stand helplessly before the spirit at bay;

if this should be, i say if this should be—
you of my heart, send me a little word;
that i may go unto him, and take his hands,
saying, Accept all happiness from me.
Then shall i turn my face, and hear one bird
sing terribly afar in the lost lands.

e. e. cummings

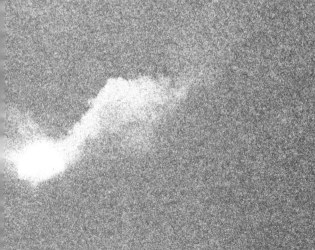

I am by nature conventional and straightforward, but Yün was a stickler for forms, like the Confucian schoolmasters. Whenever I put on a dress for her or tidied up her sleeves, she would say 'So much obliged' again and again, and when I passed her a trowel or a fan, she must receive it standing up. At first I disliked this and said to her: 'Do you mean to tie me down with all this ceremony? There is a proverb which says, "One who is overcourteous is crafty." ' Yün blushed all over and said: 'I am merely trying to be polite and respectful; why do you charge me with craftiness?' 'True respect is in the heart, and does not require such empty forms,' said I, but Yün said, 'There is no more intimate relationship than that between children and their parents. Do you mean to say that children should behave freely towards their parents and keep their respect only in their heart?' 'Oh! I was only joking,' I said. 'The trouble is,' said Yün, 'most marital troubles begin with joking. Don't you accuse me of disrespect later, for then I shall die of grief without being able to defend myself.' Then I held her close to my breast and caressed her and then she smiled. From then on our conversations were full of "I'm sorry's" and "I beg your pardon's." And so we remained courteous to each other for twenty-three years of our married life like Liang Hung and Meng Kuang of old, and the longer we stayed together,

the more passionately attached we became to each other. Whenever we met each other in the house, whether it be in a dark room or in a narrow corridor, we used to hold each other's hands and ask: "Where are you going?" and we did this on the sly as if afraid that people might see us. As a matter of fact, we tried at first to avoid being seen sitting or walking together, but after a while, we did not mind it any more. When Yün was sitting and talking with somebody and saw me come, she would rise and move sideways for me to sit down together with her. All this was done naturally almost without any consciousness, and although at first we felt uneasy about it, later on it became a matter of habit. I cannot understand why all old couples must hate each other like enemies. Some people say "if they weren't enemies, they would not be able to live together until old age." Well, I wonder!

Shen Fu, extract from 'Wedded Bliss'

WHEN A BELOVED HAND

When a belovèd hand is laid in ours,
When, jaded with the rush and glare
Of the interminable hours,
Our eyes can in another's eyes read clear,
When our world-deafened ear
Is by the tones of a loved voice caressed, –
A bolt is shot back somewhere in our breast,
And a lost pulse of feeling stirs again.
The eye sinks inward, and the heart lies plain,
And what we mean, we say, and what we would, we
    know!
A man becomes aware of his life's flow,

And hears its winding murmur, and he sees
The meadows where it glides, the sun, the breeze.

And there arrives a lull in the hot race,
Wherein he doth for ever chase
That flying and elusive shadow, rest.

An air of coolness plays upon his face,
And an unwonted calm pervades his breast.
And then he thinks he knows
The hills where his life rose,
And the sea where it goes.

Matthew Arnold

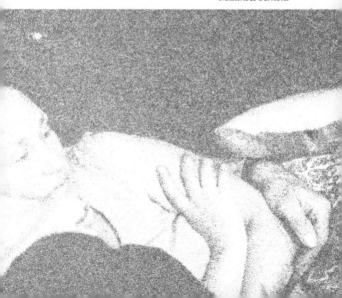

WINSTON TO CLEMENTINE CHURCHILL

You ought to trust me for I do not love and will
never love any woman in the world but you, and
my chief desire is to link myself to you week by
week by bonds which shall ever become more
intimate and profound. Beloved I kiss your
memory – your sweetness and beauty have cast a
glory upon my life. You will find me always
　　　　Your loving and
　　　　devoted husband W

Winston Churchill

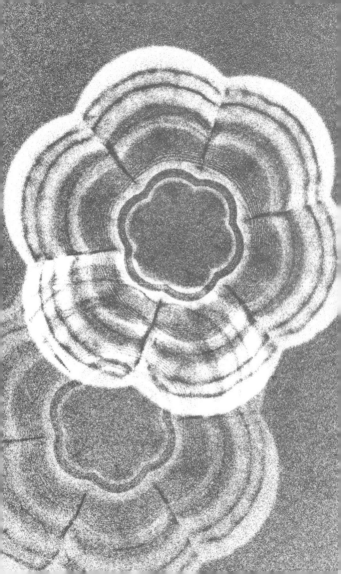

And man and woman are like the earth, that brings
    forth flowers
in summer, and love, but underneath is rock.
Older than flowers, older than ferns, older than
    foraminiferae
older than plasm altogether is the soul of a man
    underneath.

And when, throughout all the wild orgasms of love
slowly a gem forms, in the ancient, once-more-
    molten rocks
of two human hearts, two ancient rocks, a man's
    heart and a woman's,
that is the crystal of peace, the slow hard jewel of
    trust,
the sapphire of fidelity.
The gem of mutual peace emerging from the wild
    chaos of love.

D. H. Lawrence, from 'Fidelity'

NOT WHOLLY LOST

John warns me of nostalgia
And I suppose he's right – but what the hell –
What are poems for but for celebration
Of our time on the earth the years behind us
And ahead? And I for one will leave
The future to others and plunge back gladly
Into the mist of old ghosts and places
Where these appear –

                    scarlet flame of Dosco's
Open hearth behind the jail, stench of the coke-ovens,
Poverty naked as the Newfie girl under the cheap dress
That November. Smell of fish and ocean
At the North Sydney piers. Lobsters on the half-shell
In Cormier's, the movie where a hundred was a crowd.
   And on from Shediac
The warm sands, blue waters of the Point; summer that
   seemed over
Before it had begun, and our youth with it, for that year
   anyway: but there was another year
And another summer (thank God there was always
   another). Remember, we never found any clams
But drank that bottle of rum sitting on the shell-heavy
   sand of Batouche
And came back hungry to camp.

                    O what better days
were there

Than mornings on the Bournemouth cliffs, blue above
    and blue below, each outshining
The other. Or nights walking Yorkshire roads, great trees
    on either side, good smell
Of hay in the fields.
                       We would never do the things now
We did then, we've grown older, too serious; and what we
    did
For the plain simple hell of it we will not do now or in any
    other year. But we did them once,
Those things are not wholly lost; they linger in the heart,
    in the mind,
And nothing can take them from us or change them
Unless it is death.

Raymond Souster

TOUCH

and no sound
and no word spoken
and the window pane
grey in dwindling light
and no word spoken
but touch, your touch
upon my hand veined
by the changing years
that gave and took away
yet gave a touch
that took away
the years between
and brought to this grey day
the brightness we had seen
before the years had grown between.

George Bruce

John and Annie Denver

ANNIE'S SONG

You fill up my senses like a night in a forest
Like the mountains in Springtime, like a walk in the rain
Like a storm on the desert, like a sleepy blue ocean
You fill up my senses, come fill me again.

Come let me love you, let me give my life to you
Let me drown in your laughter, let me die in your arms
Let me lay down beside you, let me always be with you
Come let me love you, come love me again.

John Denver

ACKNOWLEDGEMENTS: The publishers gratefully acknowledge permission to reproduce copyright material. Every effort has been made to trace copyright holders, but in a few cases this has proved impossible. The publishers would be interested to hear from any copyright holders not here acknowledged.

DANNIE ABSE, 'Epithalamion' from *Walking Under Water*. Reprinted by permission of Anthony Sheil Associates Ltd; GEORGE BRUCE, 'Touch', from *Collected Poems*, Edinburgh University Press. Reprinted by permission of the author; JIM BURNS, 'A Single Flower' reprinted by permission of the author; WINSTON CHURCHILL, 'Letter to his wife', reprinted by permission of C. & T. Publications Ltd; E. E. CUMMINGS, 'it may not always be so; and i say', reprinted from *Tulips & Chimneys* by permission of Liveright Publishing Corporation and Granada Publishing Ltd. Copyright © 1923, 1925 and renewed 1951, 1953 by e. e. cummings. Copyright © 1973, 1976 by Nancy T. Andrews © 1973, 1976 by George James Firmage. 'i carry your heart with me (i carry it in', copyright 1952 by e. e. cummings. Reprinted from his volume *Complete Poems 1913-1962* by permission of Harcourt Brace Jovanovich, Inc. and *Complete Poems 1936-1962* Granada Publishing Ltd; JOHN DENVER, 'Annie's Song'. Reprinted by permission of Cherry Lane Music Publishing Co., Inc; T. S. ELIOT, 'A Dedication to My Wife', from *Collected Poems 1909-1962*; copyright © 1959, 1963 by Thomas Stearns Eliot. Reprinted by permission of Harcourt Brace Jovanovich, Inc., and Farrar, Straus & Giroux, Inc. and Faber and Faber Ltd; SHEN FU, Excerpt from 'Wedded Bliss', from *The Wisdom of China and India* edited by Lin Yutang. Reprinted by permission of Random House, Inc; ROBERT GRAVES, 'A Slice of Wedding Cake' and 'Gift of Sight', from *Collected Poems, 1975* published by Cassell Limited. Reprinted by permission of the author and A. P. Watt Ltd; OSCAR HAMMERSTEIN II, 'Can't Help Lovin' Dat Man', from *Showboat* Music by Jerome Kern. Copyright © 1927 by T. B. Harms Company copyright renewed. (c/o The Welk Music Group, Santa Monica, C.A. 90401) International Copyright Secured. Used by permission of T. B. Harms and Chappell Music Ltd; T. HARRI JONES, 'A Birthday Poem for Madeleine', from *Collected Poems*. Reprinted by permission of J. D. Lewis & Sons Ltd, Gomer Press; ADRIAN HENRI, 'Who?', from *Penguin Modern Poets 10*, copyright © 1967 by Adrian Henri. Used by permission of Deborah Rogers Ltd, London; ION HOREA, 'For You', from *Anthology of Contemporary Romanian Poetry*, edited and translated by Roy MacGregor-Hastie, and published by Peter Owen Ltd, London; BRIAN JONES, 'Husband to Wife: Party Going'. Reprinted by permission of London Magazine, Alan Ross Ltd; ERICA JONG, 'Living Happily Ever After'. Reprinted by permission of Sterling Lord Agency, Inc., © 1977 by Erica Jong; D. H. LAWRENCE, 'Fidelity' and 'Trust', from *The Complete Poems of D. H. Lawrence*, edited and with an Introduction and Notes by Vivian de Sola Pinto and F. Warren Roberts, published by William Heinemann Ltd. Copyright © 1964, 1971 by Angelo Ravagli and C. M. Weekley, Executors of the Estate of Frieda Lawrence Ravagli. Reprinted by permission of Viking Penguin Inc. and Lawrence Pollinger Limited, and The Estate of Frieda Lawrence Ravagli; JOHN LENNON, 'Woman', copyright 1980 Lenono, all rights reserved; LENNON AND McCARTNEY, 'Help!', reprinted by permission of the composers and Northern Songs Ltd, London; ROGER McGOUGH, 'Happiness', copyright 1973 by the author, from *Gig*, published by Cape 1973. Reprinted by permission of the author and publishers; OGDEN NASH, 'I Do, I Will, I Have', and 'The Cuckoo' from *Verses From 1929 On*. Copyright 1948 by The Curtis Publishing Company.

Copyright renewed 1975 by Frances Nash, Linell Nash Smith and Isabel Nash Eberstadt. Reprinted by permission of Little, Brown and Company and Curtis Brown Ltd. 'The Cuckoo' from *Verses From 1929 On*, copyright 1950 by Ogden Nash. First appeared in *The New Yorker*); EUGENE O'NEILL, 'A Quiet Song in Time of Chaos', from *Poems 1912-1944* edited by Donald Gallup. Copyright © 1979 by YaleUniversity. Reprinted by permission of Ticknor and Fields, Houghton Mifflin Company, Jonathan Cape Ltd. and The Executors of the Eugene O'Neill Estate; JOHN ORMOND, 'In September', reprinted by permission of the author; BRIAN PATTEN, 'A Love Poem', from *Love Poems (Vanishing Trick)*, published by George Allen & Unwin Ltd; ROBIN RAY or an unknown author, an extract from *Time for Lovers*, published by Weidenfeld (Publishers) Limited; RUFINOS from *Classical Epigrams — Love and Wit*, translated by André Lefevere, published by Studio Vista, a division of Cassell Limited; BERTRAND RUSSELL, 'Love an escape from loneliness', from *Marriage & Morals*. Reprinted by permission of Liveright Publishing Corporation and George Allen & Unwin. Copyright 1929 by Horace Liveright, Inc. Copyright © 1957 by Bertrand Russell; GEORGE BERNARD SHAW, Extract from *Man and Superman (Maxims for Revolutionists)*. Reprinted by permission of The Society of Authors on behalf of the Bernard Shaw Estate; RAYMOND SOUSTER, 'Not Wholly Lost, from *Collected Souster Volume 1*. Reprinted by permission of Oberon Press, Ottawa, Canada; BERNARD SPENCER, 'Part of Plenty', reprinted by permission of Alan Ross Ltd; DYLAN THOMAS, Extract from *Under Milk Wood*, published by J. M. Dent. Reprinted by permission of David Higham Associates Ltd; PAUL WILLIAMS, 'That's Enough For Me', reprinted by Rondor Music (London) Ltd.

PHOTOGRAPHS:
BRUCE ATKINS, Photograph illustrating 'i carry your heart'; PETER BEHRENS, Photograph of 'Der Kuss' illustrating 'Rufinos'; FRANCES BERRILL, Photograms illustrating 'Not Wholly Lost', 'Fidelity' and 'A Single Flower'; BILL BRANDT, Photograph from '*Shadow of Light*' illustrating 'Living Happily Ever After'; RICHARD BRAINE/SOURCE, Photograph illustrating 'Gift of Sight'; SHAWNA EASTON, Photograph illustrating 'Touch'; ELISABETH PHOTO LIBRARY, Photograph illustrating 'I Do, I Will, I Have'; MARY EVANS PICTURE LIBRARY, Photograph illustrating 'Trust' and the cover illustration; RICHARD EXLEY, Photographs illustrating 'A Quiet Song in Time of Chaos', 'Part of Plenty', 'A Slice of Wedding Cake', 'A Dedication to my Wife', 'Happiness', 'Epithalamion', 'Who?', 'Quiet Song in Time of Chaos' and the extract from *Under Milk Wood*; GORDON GUMN, Photograph illustrating 'The Prophet'; SYLVESTER JACOBS, Photographs illustrating 'Husband to Wife: Party Going' and 'Can't Help Lovin' dat Man'; CAMILLA JESSEL, Photograph illustrating 'A Birthday Poem For Madeleine'; MICHAEL JOSEPH, Photograph illustrating 'In September'; PAUL KAYE, Photograph illustrating 'When a Beloved Hand'; KENNEDY/SOURCE, Photograph illustrating 'it may not always be so'; KEYSTONE PRESS, Photograph illustrating 'That's Enough For Me' and 'Romance'; POPPERFOTO, Photograph illustrating 'let me not to the marriage . . .' and 'Help'; CLARE SCHWOB, Photograph illustrating poem by Ion Horea; JOHN TOPHAM PICTURE LIBRARY, Letter from Winston Churchill; VERLAG GALERIE WEIZ SALSBURG, 'The Kiss' by Gustav Klimt illustrating poem by Rubén Dario.